An Authors Book for WIPs

Working Title: _______________________

Genre: _______________________

Quick Plot Line: _______________________

____

____

____

Notes

____
____
____
____
____
____
____
____
____
____
____
____
____
____

WORKING TITLE: _______________________________

GENRE: _______________________________

QUICK PLOT LINE: _______________________________

____

____

____

NOTES

____

____

____

____

____

____

____

____

____

____

____

____

____

____

____

____

Working Title: ___________________________

Genre: ___________________________

Quick Plot Line: ___________________________

____

____

____

Notes

____

____

____

____

____

____

____

____

____

____

____

____

____

____

____

____

____

Working Title: ___________________________________

Genre: ___________________________________

Quick Plot Line: ___________________________________

____

____

____

Notes

____

____

____

____

____

____

____

____

____

____

____

____

____

____

____

Working Title:

Genre:

Quick Plot Line:

Notes

Working Title:

Genre:

Quick Plot Line:

Notes

WORKING TITLE:

GENRE:

QUICK PLOT LINE:

NOTES

WORKING TITLE: ______________________________

GENRE: ______________________________

QUICK PLOT LINE: ______________________________

____

____

____

NOTES

____
____
____
____
____
____
____
____
____
____
____
____
____
____
____
____

Working Title:

Genre:

Quick Plot Line:

Notes

Working Title: ______________________________

Genre: ______________________________

Quick Plot Line: ______________________________

____

____

____

NOTES

Working Title: ______________________________

Genre: ______________________________

Quick Plot Line: ______________________________

____

____

____

Notes

Working Title:

Genre:

Quick Plot Line:

Notes

WORKING TITLE: ______________________________

GENRE: ______________________________

QUICK PLOT LINE: ______________________________

____

____

____

NOTES

____

____

____

____

____

____

____

____

____

____

____

____

____

____

____

____

Working Title:

Genre:

Quick Plot Line:

Notes

WORKING TITLE:

GENRE:

QUICK PLOT LINE:

NOTES

Working Title:

Genre:

Quick Plot Line:

Notes

Working Title:

Genre:

Quick Plot Line:

Notes

Working Title: _______________________________________

Genre: _______________________________________

Quick Plot Line: _______________________________________

____

____

____

Notes

____

____

____

____

____

____

____

____

____

____

____

____

____

____

____

____

____

Working Title:

Genre:

Quick Plot Line:

Notes

WORKING TITLE:

GENRE:

QUICK PLOT LINE:

NOTES

Working Title:

Genre:

Quick Plot Line:

Notes

Working Title:

Genre:

Quick Plot Line:

Notes

Working Title: ____________________________

Genre: ____________________________

Quick Plot Line: ____________________________

Notes

Working Title:

Genre:

Quick Plot Line:

Notes

Working Title:

Genre:

Quick Plot Line:

Notes

WORKING TITLE:

GENRE:

QUICK PLOT LINE:

NOTES

WORKING TITLE: ____

GENRE: ____

QUICK PLOT LINE: ____

____

____

____

NOTES

Working Title:

Genre:

Quick Plot Line:

Notes

Working Title: ___________________________

Genre: ___________________________

Quick Plot Line: ___________________________

____

____

____

Notes

____

Working Title:

Genre:

Quick Plot Line:

Notes

Working Title:

Genre:

Quick Plot Line:

Notes

WORKING TITLE: _______________________

GENRE: _______________________

QUICK PLOT LINE: _______________________

____

____

____

NOTES

Working Title: _______________________________

Genre: _______________________________

Quick Plot Line: _______________________________

____

____

____

Notes

____

____

____

____

____

____

____

____

____

____

____

____

____

____

Working Title: _______________________________

Genre: _______________________________

Quick Plot Line: _______________________________

____

____

____

Notes

____

____

____

____

____

____

____

____

____

____

____

____

____

____

____

Working Title:

Genre:

Quick Plot Line:

Notes

WORKING TITLE:

GENRE:

QUICK PLOT LINE:

NOTES

Working Title: _______________________________

Genre: _______________________________

Quick Plot Line: _______________________________

____

____

____

Notes

____

____

____

____

____

____

____

____

____

____

____

____

____

Working Title: ____

Genre: ____

Quick Plot Line: ____

____

____

____

Notes

____

____

____

____

____

____

____

____

____

____

____

____

____

____

____

____

Working Title:

Genre:

Quick Plot Line:

Notes

WORKING TITLE:

GENRE:

QUICK PLOT LINE:

NOTES

Working Title:

Genre:

Quick Plot Line:

Notes

Working Title: ______________________________

Genre: ______________________________

Quick Plot Line: ______________________________

____

____

____

Notes

____

____

____

____

____

____

____

____

____

____

____

____

____

____

____

____

____

Working Title:

Genre:

Quick Plot Line:

Notes

Working Title: _______________________

Genre: _______________________

Quick Plot Line: _______________________

____

____

____

Notes

Working Title:

Genre:

Quick Plot Line:

Notes

Working Title: ____

Genre: ____

Quick Plot Line: ____

____

____

____

Notes

____

____

____

____

____

____

____

____

____

____

____

____

____

____

WORKING TITLE:

GENRE:

QUICK PLOT LINE:

NOTES

Working Title: ______________________________

Genre: ______________________________

Quick Plot Line: ______________________________

____

____

____

NOTES

____

____

____

____

____

____

____

____

____

____

____

____

____

WORKING TITLE:

GENRE:

QUICK PLOT LINE:

NOTES

Working Title: _______________________________

Genre: _______________________________

Quick Plot Line: _______________________________

____

____

____

Notes

Working Title:

Genre:

Quick Plot Line:

Notes

Working Title:

Genre:

Quick Plot Line:

Notes

Working Title: __________________________

Genre: __________________________

Quick Plot Line: __________________________

____

____

____

Notes

____

____

____

____

____

____

____

____

____

____

____

____

____

Working Title:

Genre:

Quick Plot Line:

Notes

Notes

Working Title: ___________________________

Genre: ___________________________

Quick Plot Line: ___________________________

____

____

____

Notes

WORKING TITLE:

GENRE:

QUICK PLOT LINE:

NOTES

Working Title:

Genre:

Quick Plot Line:

Notes

WORKING TITLE:

GENRE:

QUICK PLOT LINE:

NOTES

Working Title:

Genre:

Quick Plot Line:

Notes

WORKING TITLE:

GENRE:

QUICK PLOT LINE:

NOTES

Working Title:

Genre:

Quick Plot Line:

Notes

Working Title:

Genre:

Quick Plot Line:

Notes

Working Title:

Genre:

Quick Plot Line:

Notes

WORKING TITLE:

GENRE:

QUICK PLOT LINE:

NOTES

Working Title:

Genre:

Quick Plot Line:

Notes

Working Title: _______________________________

Genre: _______________________________

Quick Plot Line: _______________________________

____

____

____

Notes

____

____

____

____

____

____

____

____

____

____

____

____

____

____

____

WORKING TITLE: ____

GENRE: ____

QUICK PLOT LINE: ____

____

____

____

NOTES

WORKING TITLE:

GENRE:

QUICK PLOT LINE:

NOTES

WORKING TITLE:

GENRE:

QUICK PLOT LINE:

NOTES

Working Title:

Genre:

Quick Plot Line:

Notes

Working Title:

Genre:

Quick Plot Line:

Notes

WORKING TITLE:

GENRE:

QUICK PLOT LINE:

NOTES

Notes

WORKING TITLE:

GENRE:

QUICK PLOT LINE:

NOTES

Working Title:

Genre:

Quick Plot Line:

Notes

Working Title: _______________________

Genre: _______________________

Quick Plot Line: _______________________

____

____

____

Notes

____

____

____

____

____

____

____

____

____

____

____

____

____

____

____

WORKING TITLE:

GENRE:

QUICK PLOT LINE:

NOTES

WORKING TITLE:

GENRE:

QUICK PLOT LINE:

NOTES

Working Title:

Genre:

Quick Plot Line:

Notes

WORKING TITLE:

GENRE:

QUICK PLOT LINE:

NOTES

Working Title: _______________________

Genre: _______________________

Quick Plot Line: _______________________

____

____

____

Notes

WORKING TITLE:

GENRE:

QUICK PLOT LINE:

NOTES

WORKING TITLE:

GENRE:

QUICK PLOT LINE:

NOTES

WORKING TITLE:

GENRE:

QUICK PLOT LINE:

NOTES

WORKING TITLE: ____

GENRE: ____

QUICK PLOT LINE: ____

NOTES

Working Title: _______________________

Genre: _______________________

Quick Plot Line: _______________________

____

____

____

Notes

WORKING TITLE: _______________________________

GENRE: _______________________________

QUICK PLOT LINE: _______________________________

____

____

____

NOTES

____

____

____

____

____

____

____

____

____

____

____

____

____

WORKING TITLE:

GENRE:

QUICK PLOT LINE:

NOTES

Working Title: _______________________________

Genre: _______________________________

Quick Plot Line: _______________________________

____

____

____

Notes

____
____
____
____
____
____
____
____
____
____
____
____
____
____
____
____

Working Title: ___________________________

Genre: ___________________________

Quick Plot Line: ___________________________

____

____

____

Notes

WORKING TITLE:

GENRE:

QUICK PLOT LINE:

NOTES

Working Title: ______________________________

Genre: ______________________________

Quick Plot Line: ______________________________

____

____

____

Notes

____

____

____

____

____

____

____

____

____

____

____

____

____

____

Working Title: ______________________________

Genre: ______________________________

Quick Plot Line: ______________________________

____

____

____

Notes

____

____

____

____

____

____

____

____

____

____

____

____

____

____

____

Working Title: _______________________

Genre: _______________________

Quick Plot Line: _______________________

____

____

____

Notes

____

____

____

____

____

____

____

____

____

____

____

____

____

____

____

Working Title:

Genre:

Quick Plot Line:

Notes

Working Title:

Genre:

Quick Plot Line:

Notes

Working Title: _______________________

Genre: _______________________

Quick Plot Line: _______________________

____

____

____

Notes

____

____

____

____

____

____

____

____

____

____

____

____

____

____

____

____

____

Working Title: _______________________

Genre: _______________________

Quick Plot Line: _______________________

____

____

____

Notes

____

Working Title:

Genre:

Quick Plot Line:

Notes

Thank you so much for your purchase.

I really do hope that this book has helped you,
even in some small way.

Would you like to see different designs/styles?

I am always very happy to hear from customers,
so please feel free to email me on

teeceedesignstudio@yahoo.com